W9-DGT-251

ROYAL HOMES

BUCKINGHAM PALACE SEEN ACROSS ST JAMES'S PARK

ROYAL HOMES

BUCKINGHAM PALACE

WINDSOR CASTLE

THE PALACE OF HOLYROODHOUSE

ST JAMES'S PALACE

CLARENCE HOUSE

BALMORAL CASTLE

SANDRINGHAM HOUSE

BY GORDON NARES

COUNTRY LIFE LIMITED

2-10 TAVISTOCK STREET COVENT GARDEN LONDON WC2

Published in 1953

by Country Life Limited

Tavistock Street London WC2

Printed and bound in England by

Hazell, Watson & Viney Ltd

Aylesbury and London

CONTENTS

Plates are referred to in italic type

ACKNOWLEDGMENTS

A NUMBER of works have been consulted in the preparation of this volume, but I am particularly indebted to *Buckingham Palace* (1930), by Mr H. Clifford Smith, *Windsor Castle* (1951), by Sir Owen Morshead, and *Clarence House* (1949), by Mr Christopher Hussey.

The following photographs are reproduced by gracious permission of Her Majesty The Queen: of Buckingham Palace, the reproduction of Blore's water-colour on page 14; of Windsor Castle, the photographs on page 45, and on pages 54 to 81; of the Palace of Holyroodhouse, the photographs on pages 87 to 91.

Acknowledgments are also due to the following for other photographs reproduced in this book:

G. F. Allen: frontispiece, and pages 15, 47, 52, 53; Aerofilms Ltd: pages 16, 17, 42, 84, 93 (top), 107; Central Press Photos Ltd: page 43; Logan's Studios: pages 46, 48 (bottom), 49 (bottom); George Spearman: pages 48 (top), 49 (top), 51; 'Picture Post': page 50; Valentine & Sons Ltd: pages 82, 86, 106, 108, 109 (top), 110; The Travel Association: page 83 (top); J. Allan Cash: pages 83 (bottom), 85; Wm. S. Thomson: page 109 (bottom); Fox Photos: page 112.

G. N.

INTRODUCTION

MOST of the residences of the British Kings and Queens have had the character of country houses rather than of palaces. They have been intended to afford the Sovereign relaxation from cares of State rather than to contain a Court or impress the representatives of other countries. Before George IV rebuilt Windsor Castle and Buckingham Palace, there was no Royal residence that could compare for architectural dignity with such great Continental palaces as Versailles, Tsarskoye Selo, Schönbrunn or Caserta, and they were outshone even by some of our great country houses. 'We have nothing like this', commented George III when he visited the Duke and Duchess of Marlborough at Blenheim Palace in 1786.

This comparative modesty has not been due to lack of interest in building or want of taste on the part of many of our kings. Those who ruled wisely saw that their subjects' affection counted for more than stately building; and those who were less well advised were prone to discover that Parliament and public opinion did not favour a grand manner of living. Those with expensive tastes—Henry III, Charles I, Charles II, George IV—have not been remembered in history as the best of kings. Consequently those who have reigned longest and most successfully were content with adapting, enlarging or embellishing old palaces rather than building new ones.

This was also true of the mediæval kings, whose palaces had to serve for defence as well as administration, but little of their building survives except Windsor, the Tower of London and the name of the Palace of Westminster. Even Henry VIII, who could have built himself a Fontainebleau, usually restricted himself to building where others had built before—at Whitehall, Hampton Court and St James's—rather than to starting afresh. Nonsuch Palace, in Surrey, was his most ambitious venture and would have been of great interest as an example of Tudor taste, but it was pulled down in the seventeenth century. Queen Elizabeth I was too wise and economical to spend her people's money on building houses instead of ships. Of the Stuart kings, fate decreed that William III alone was in a financial position to enhance the dignity of the Crown with architecture at will. He employed Sir Christopher Wren to build the magnificent State Apartments at Hampton Court and the homelier but nevertheless beautiful palace at Kensington. Neither of these, however, is still in use as a palace.

All that is most admirable in those occupied as residences today is almost entirely due to two kings. Both Charles II and George IV were influenced by the example of their Continental contemporaries, and both overcame a chronic shortage of funds in pursuit of their love of building. George IV, moreover, whatever his shortcomings, was an enthusiastic patron of architects, artists and craftsmen, and he exercised a far-reaching influence on the visual arts. His fostering of 'the spirit of metropolitan improvement' transformed the appearance of London, and the character that he impressed on his residences brought them on to a level with eighteenth-century European standards.

The palaces for which Charles II and George IV were mainly responsible—together at St James's and Windsor, singly at Holyroodhouse and Buckingham Palace—are now, as a result of their efforts, great national monuments. But the country-house tradition inspiring so many of their predecessors was, and still is, maintained by Balmoral and Sandringham, both of which were acquired and built under the influence of Queen Victoria and Prince Albert. The products of that era, as of others, have not been continuously admired, but the time has come when they seem to merit more appreciation, and perhaps revaluation, and there is every sign that the process has already begun.

In the following pages no attempt has been made to give more than an outline of the history of Balmoral, Sandringham and Clarence House, for they are essentially private houses and merit the respect for privacy that is accorded to the houses of ordinary citizens. More space has been devoted to St James's Palace and Holyroodhouse, however: the former because its interior is little known to the general public and the latter as it is the official Royal residence in Scotland. But the greater part of the book is concerned with Windsor Castle and Buckingham Palace, and their interiors have been described and illustrated in considerable detail, for this year they will play an enhanced rôle in the life of the Nation—the one as the historic seat from which the Royal Family takes its name, and the other as the hub of London and symbol of a Commonwealth, to which the Queen's subjects flock to acclaim her at the Coronation.

G. N.

BUCKINGHAM PALACE

EARLY in his reign James I conceived the idea of starting a silk industry in this country, and on November 29, 1609, he paid a man called Stallenge £935, which was his estimate for planting a four-acre mulberry garden adjoining the west side of St James's Park. The silk industry never materialized, the silk worms disappeared and the mulberry trees eventually died, but the small plot of land remained in Royal hands and it forms the nucleus of the forty-acre garden in which Buckingham Palace stands today.

Charles I leased the little walled mulberry garden and the buildings on it to Lord Aston, whose son sold the lease to Lord Goring, the 'courtly, magnificent and extravagant' Cavalier. Goring extended the mulberry garden by buying twenty acres to the west of it, known as Goring Great Garden, and on part of the site was built Goring House—Buckingham Palace's great-grandparent. It was rebuilt by Lord Arlington, after whom it was called Arlington House, and then it was bought by John Sheffield, who in 1703 was created Duke of Buckingham; the name and the place are at last associated.

The new Duke pulled down Arlington House and rebuilt it, partly on his own freehold land—formerly Goring Great Garden—and partly on the Crown leasehold land—the old mulberry garden—with blithe disregard for what would happen when the lease ultimately reverted to the Crown. The new Buckingham House was designed by Captain William Winde, and was a three-storeyed building of brick with stone pilasters, connected by curved colonnades to flanking pavilions.

The Duke of Buckingham died in 1721, and left the house and its grounds to his Duchess, who believed herself to be an illegitimate daughter of James II and lived there in semi-royal state with an army of retainers, ladies-in-waiting and a Jacobite Court. Nevertheless, George II, when Prince of Wales, tried to buy or lease Buckingham House from her, and she is said to have bargained with 'the haughtiness of a Jacobite and the astuteness of an Estate Agent'. Nothing came of the deal, presumably because the price she asked was exorbitant. She died in 1742, and eventually Buckingham House fell to an illegitimate son of the first Duke, Charles Herbert. The folly of his father's building the house partly on leasehold and partly on freehold land soon became apparent, for the time when the lease of the old mulberry garden would be reclaimed by the Crown was drawing near. He attempted to renew the lease, but he was persuaded in 1762 to sell

the freehold portion of the property to George III. The agreement was signed on April 20, 1763, and thus the Royal connection with the site, so tenuously maintained since 1609, became absolute. George III bought Buckingham House as a dower house for Queen Caroline—he always referred to it as the Queen's House—and it continued to be used as the Royal Family's private London residence until her death in 1818.

Two years later her son, George IV, came to the throne, and it soon became obvious that he wished to build or at least rebuild himself a London home. The accommodation at Carlton House was insufficient and, indeed, the structure was evidently unsafe, for 'whenever a large assembly was held in the upper rooms it became necessary to prop up the lower ones', and 'far from His Majesty wishing to leave that house, the house seemed disposed to leave His Majesty'. Moreover, as he himself said: 'I do not like Carlton House standing in a street'. His architect, John Nash, began to draw up plans for enlarging Buckingham House and alternatively for building an entirely new palace, but the King insisted that he wanted only what he called a 'pied-à-terre', and furthermore that it should be at Buckingham House.

So, in 1825, work was begun. The shell of the old house was kept and converted into the State Apartments, but it was considerably extended to north and south, giving a long façade facing west to the gardens. In the centre of this front was added a bow surmounted by a dome, and the skyline was enlivened by four attic pavilions. On the east front, facing St James's Park, an entrance portico of two storeys with coupled Corinthian columns was erected, and two long low wings embraced the forecourt, at the eastern end of which were columned pavilions. At right angles to these wings were screen walls with Doric colonnades, which, like the portico, survive to this day. Facing the portico at the entrance to the forecourt was placed the Marble Arch.

From the first, Nash's building was badly received, although the criticisms were perhaps prompted largely by the politics of the time. The flanking wings were said to be too low and the dome came in for some well-merited abuse. It was too small to dominate the west front, but just large enough to be seen from the east peeping above the roof like a 'wretched inverted egg-cup'. The wings were almost immediately rebuilt with their roof-line level with that of the body of the Palace; this greatly increased the accommodation, but did not improve the appearance of the forecourt and detracted from the effect of the main block.

In addition to these æsthetic troubles, there were practical difficulties. The King and his architect grossly overspent the money allotted by Parliament for rebuilding Buckingham House, and in 1828 a Select Committee was appointed to enquire into 'the State of Public Buildings in the Department of the Office of Works'. As a result of the enquiry the House of Commons limited the amount which could be spent on completing the Palace, but meanwhile the King had told Nash that 'the State Rooms you have made me are so handsome that I think I shall hold my Courts there', and, with the idea of turning his *pied-à-terre* into a palace, he began to give his architect orders involving heavy additional expense. In June 1830, George IV died, leaving the Palace unfinished, the finances in chaos, and his architect in trouble with another Select Committee.

When William IV succeeded to the throne it was rumoured that he intended to sell the incomplete Palace. Instead, he decided to finish it, and Edward Blore was commissioned to prepare plans. Most of his work consisted in doing what Nash had left undone, but in one respect he materially altered his predecessor's design. Partly to provide extra bedroom accommodation, and partly to mask Nash's offending dome and attic pavilions on the west front, he raised the main block of the building by one storey. The pavilions disappeared and the dome became a half-dome. The additional storey was altogether a success on the west front, which has been described as 'one of the most charming examples of late classic architecture in the country', but on the entrance front it does not appear to such advantage, since it detracts from the effect of Nash's noble portico. In May 1837, Buckingham Palace was at last finished—and within a month the King was dead.

Queen Victoria occupied Buckingham Palace almost immediately after her accession, but before long the building—for all the money that had been spent on it—was found to be too small for a married Sovereign. A few minor alterations were made in 1841 in preparation for the young Queen's wedding, but within five years she was writing to Sir Robert Peel of 'the total want of accommodation for our family, which is fast growing up'. Consequently, in 1846, Blore drew up plans for filling in the open (east) side of the courtyard and for rebuilding the south wing. The building of the new front necessitated the removal of the Marble Arch, which was eventually transplanted to its familiar position on the north side of Hyde Park, and in its place rose Blore's many-windowed façade. The architect's task was admittedly difficult, being to provide an imposing entrance front, yet containing rooms of only secondary importance, but the result could not be described as anything but dull.

Blore was followed by James Pennethorne, who was trained in the office of John Nash. His principal contribution to the Palace was the Ball Room, which stands up above the rest of the building in the south-west corner. When his work was complete, Queen Victoria was able to transfer the Drawing Rooms and other Court functions from St James's to Buckingham Palace.

But the Palace was not yet as we see it. In 1913 it was decided that a more impressive backdrop to the new Victoria Memorial was needed than Blore's east façade, the stonework of which was decaying badly. The new east front was designed by Sir Aston Webb, who was responsible also for the Admiralty Arch at the Trafalgar Square end of the Mall. Although the new front is little more inspired than the one it replaced—Mr John Summerson has called it a 'bold platitude'—it provides a dignified frontispiece to the Palace. Sir Aston's task was complicated by having to retain Blore's openings and fenestration, and the refacing was done without even removing the glass from the windows.

The Palace is entered from the forecourt through the trio of arches in the east front, which give into the courtyard. On the right, in the north wing, are the Private Apartments of the Royal Family; the south side is occupied chiefly by the Officers of the Household. Facing is Nash's Grand Entrance. Let us assume that we have the entrée to the Palace and can pass under the portico and into the Grand Hall, which occupies the position of the entrance hall of old Buckingham House. Pairs of marble columns are set around the walls, and along the inner side runs the middle section of the long, wide corridor known as the Marble Hall, which traverses the length of the Palace from north to south; on a raised stage to the right is a handsome marble chimney-piece with a bust of George IV in the pediment; and on the left is the splendid Grand Staircase, decorated in white and gold and laid with a crimson carpet, by which the State Apartments on the first floor are reached.

The Grand Staircase, which is hung with full-length portraits of members of the Royal Family, divides at the first landing. A straight flight continues to the State Supper Room and Ball Room, but further flights curve up on either side to join again at the entrance to the Guard Chamber, the first of the State Apartments. It is a small oval ante-room and gives access to the Green Drawing Room, which lies above the Grand Hall and derives its name from its panels of striped green brocade. The gilt furniture is mostly of the Regency period and the portraits include members of the Royal Family during George III's reign.

The Green Drawing Room is used as an assembly room for the Throne Room, which lies beyond it to the north. Her Majesty's throne stands on a dais in the

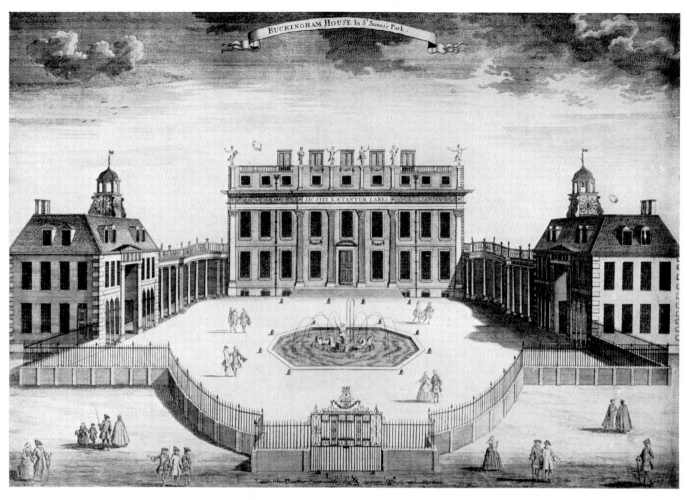

BUCKINGHAM HOUSE: AN ENGRAVING OF 1714. It shows the building designed by Captain Winde for the Duke of Buckingham in 1704 and bought by George III in 1762.

ST JAMES'S PARK IN THE REIGN OF QUEEN ANNE. Buckingham House can be seen on the left, with St James's Palace and Marlborough House in the centre.

11

Royal Alcove at the north end of this magnificent room. The alcove is framed by gilt piers, above which soar winged figures of Victory carrying garlands that support a medallion with George IV's cypher. The high, domed ceiling has a deep gilt cove, beneath which is a sculptured frieze by E. H. Baily, depicting incidents in the Wars of the Roses. The walls, once hung with panels of red silk, have since been painted a stone colour, and the deep red Brussels carpet is patterned with Tudor roses. Notable among the paintings are Allan Ramsay's Coronation portraits of George III and Queen Caroline.

These three rooms—Guard Chamber, Green Drawing Room and Throne Room—comprise the suite of State Apartments on the courtyard side of the Palace. They are separated from the range of Apartments overlooking the garden on the west front by the Picture Gallery and the Silk Tapestry Room, both of which are lit from above. The Picture Gallery, which is 155 feet long and 27 feet wide, contains a magnificent collection of paintings, mainly of the Dutch School, and including works by such artists as Rubens, Rembrandt, Hals, Cuyp, Ruysdael, Hobbema, Vermeer, Ter Borch, Steen, de Hooch and Wouvermanns. They were mostly acquired by King George IV.

The western range of State Apartments is entered at the north end through the Royal Closet, a small room decorated with crimson wallpaper on which hangs an assembly of Primitive paintings collected by the Prince Consort. Among the artists represented are Fra Angelico, Bellini, Perugino, Mabuse and Cranach. The marble and ormolu chimney-piece was originally designed by Henry Holland for the Throne Room at Carlton House. The Royal Closet is used as an assembly room by the Royal Family during the holding of Courts; from there the Royal procession moves down the length of the State Apartments to the Ball Room at the opposite end of the Palace.

The first room through which the procession passes is the White Drawing Room, named after its white-and-gold decoration. Beneath the rich tent-like ceiling is a series of sculptured panels by William Pitts depicting the Origin and Progress of Pleasure, and on the walls are huge mirrors which reflect the light from the five splendid cut-glass chandeliers. Among the furniture ranged around the walls are superb examples by French craftsmen of the eighteenth century.

Beyond the White Drawing Room is the Music Room, which fills the centre of the west front with its five-windowed bay. Over this projecting bay is a half-dome and above the main body of the room is a full dome. The Royal arms appear on the four pendentives, and in the three tympana between them is sculpture by William Pitts representing Harmony, Eloquence and

Pleasure. The ivory-coloured walls are divided into panels by eighteen Corinthian columns of blue scagliola, which foreshadow the vivid colouring of the next Apartment.

This is the Blue Drawing Room—the most magnificent of the State Apartments—so called after its turquoise flock wallpaper, which, together with the gilt blue-upholstered Regency furniture and crimson-and-gold Axminster carpet, provides a splendid spectacle of colour. The room is divided into two compartments, the larger of which is sub-divided into three bays, each with a shallow saucer dome, by pairs of scagliola columns in imitation of onyx. The smaller compartment provides an ante-room to the State Dining Room—the last State Apartment in this range and the only one of the series in which Nash had no hand, for it was decorated by Blore after his dismissal. The three saucer domes on the elaborate ceiling rest on vaulted coves, in which medallions bearing the cypher of William IV alternate with console brackets. Honey-coloured walls and a crimson Wilton carpet set off the handsome early-nineteenth-century furniture, but the room is dominated by the famous assemblage of full-length Royal portraits, which include George III and Queen Caroline by Gainsborough, and George IV by Lawrence.

At the south end of the State Dining Room is the West Gallery—hung with Gobelins tapestries woven with scenes from Don Quixote—from which Pennethorne's Ball Room is entered. The latter was built between 1853 and 1855, though it has since been much altered, notably in 1902, and is the largest of the State Apartments. At the west end is the throne dais, backed by Corinthian columns supporting a detached arch that culminates in a medallion depicting the heads of Queen Victoria and the Prince Consort in profile. Beneath the arch is a crimson velvet canopy, worked with the Royal arms. At the opposite end of the room a recess contains an organ, and on either side, facing across the broad expanse of parquetry floor, are tiers of seats.

Contemporary with the Ball Room were added the State Supper Room and the East Gallery, which is now hung with English eighteenth-century paintings by such artists as Gainsborough, Hoppner, Copley and Benjamin West. This gallery leads from the Ball Room to the Grand Staircase, and thus completes the circuit of the State Apartments.

Beneath the range of State Rooms overlooking the garden on the west front of the Palace is a suite of Semi-State Apartments. They are entered from the Marble Hall, which is decorated like the Grand Hall with pairs of marble columns enriched with gilt; it lies immediately underneath the Picture Gallery, and connects with it at the north end by the Ministers' Staircase, which was

THE EAST FRONT OF BUCKINGHAM PALACE AS ENVISAGED BY NASH IN 1827. The flanking wings were
later heightened and the Marble Arch placed at the entrance to the forecourt.

THE WEST FRONT IN 1831. The engraving shows the façade as completed by John Nash for George IV and before the
addition of the top storey by Edward Blore in William IV's reign.

added by Blore in 1834 and is hung with eighteenth-century Gobelins tapestries. The Semi-State Rooms include the Household Dining Room and Breakfast Room; the Bow Room, which lies under the Music Room facing the Grand Entrance; the Forty-Four Room, associated with the Emperor Nicholas of Russia's visit to England in 1844; and the Fifty-Five Room, in which hang paintings commemorating the visits of Queen Victoria to Paris and of Napoleon III and the Empress Eugénie to England in 1855.

The State and Semi-State Apartments at Buckingham Palace provide a sumptuous and regal setting for Royal functions, but in their decoration and appointments they are also a lasting monument to the partnership of a versatile architect, John Nash, and his enlightened but maligned Royal patron, King George IV.

THE EAST FRONT, WITH THE MARBLE ARCH IN ITS ORIGINAL POSITION. A water-colour by Joseph Nash, 1846. In the same year Blore designed a new east front to enclose the quadrangle.

THE EAST FRONT TODAY.   This front is due to Sir Aston Webb, who refaced Blore's original façade in 1913.

AERIAL VIEW FROM THE SOUTH-EAST. This photograph, looking down into the quadrangle, gives an admirable idea of the extent of the Palace. On the right is Sir Aston Webb's east front facing across the forecourt, where the guard is being changed. In the north front of the Palace are the Private Apartments of the Royal Family. The west front, facing across the huge lawn to the lake, contains the State Apartments, culminating at the left-hand end in the high-roofed Ball Room. In the background can be seen part of the Palace's forty-acre garden, bounded on the north by the rows of trees lining Constitution Hill.

AERIAL VIEW FROM THE WEST. Buckingham Palace in relation to London. In the foreground are the lake, lawn and Royal Mews. To the left is a corner of Green Park, and in the middle is the Mall, running eastwards from the Victoria Memorial, before the east front of the Palace, to the Admiralty Arch and Trafalgar Square. On the north side of the Mall can be seen Stafford House, Clarence House, St James's Palace, Marlborough House and Carlton House Terrace. On its south side is St James's Park, and beyond it the Admiralty buildings, Horseguards Parade and the Foreign Office.

THE ROYAL BALCONY, EAST FRONT. Here the Royal Family stands on great occasions to receive the cheers of the crowds. Beneath the balcony is the main entrance to the quadrangle.

18

THE GRAND ENTRANCE SEEN FROM ACROSS THE QUADRANGLE. The sculpture in the pediment of Nash's portico depicts Britannia.

19

THE WEST SIDE OF THE QUADRANGLE. The attic storey, containing friezes of sculpture intended for the Marble Arch, was added by Blore to Nash's original design.

THE NORTH-WEST CORNER OF THE QUADRANGLE

THE WEST, OR GARDEN, FRONT, SEEN FROM ACROSS THE LAWN. The attic storey was added by Blore, and greatly improved the appearance of this façade, which originally had a small central dome.

PERSPECTIVE VIEW OF THE WEST FRONT

THE GRAND HALL. It lies inside the Grand Entrance and occupies the site of the hall of old Buckingham House. On the left is the Grand Staircase, by which the State Apartments are reached, and on the right is the Marble Hall, which runs the length of the Palace from north to south.

22

Left: **MARBLE CHIMNEY-PIECE IN THE GRAND HALL.** In the pediment is a bust of George IV. *Right:* **CORONATION PORTRAIT OF GEORGE IV.** The painting by Sir Thomas Lawrence in the State Dining Room.

23

THE GRAND STAIRCASE. At the foot of the Staircase is the Grand Hall and at its head the entrance to the State Apartments. Flanking the door are portraits of Queen Adelaide and William IV.

THE GRAND STAIRCASE. Above the full-length portraits of members of the Royal Family are two of the series of four carved friezes depicting the seasons.

THE GREEN DRAWING ROOM. It lies above the Grand Hall, with its windows overlooking the quadrangle through the columns of the portico, and provides an ante-room to the adjoining Throne Room.

THE THRONE ROOM. On the right is the Royal Alcove. The winged figures of Victory fronting the Royal Alcove carry garlands with George IV's cypher in the middle. The sculptured frieze represents scenes from the Wars of the Roses.

27

THE ROYAL CLOSET. This is the first of the range of State Apartments on the west front. The chimney-piece came from Carlton House, and the Italian paintings were collected by the Prince Consort.

28

THE WHITE DRAWING ROOM. The room is so called for its white and gold decorations. It contains a notable assembly of French and Regency furniture.

THE MUSIC ROOM. This room stands in the middle of the west front. Round its walls are eighteen columns of blue scagliola.

THE MUSIC ROOM BOW. The five windows command a sweeping view westwards across the lawn to the lake.

31

THE BLUE DRAWING ROOM. This is the most magnificent of the State Apartments. The walls and upholstery are blue, and the ceiling is richly gilt.

THE STATE DINING ROOM. It is the last of the State Apartments on the west front and the only one in which Nash had no hand, as it was decorated after his death by Blore.

33

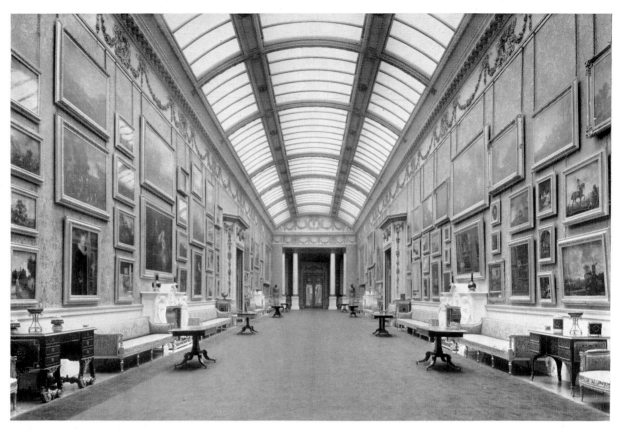

THE PICTURE GALLERY, LOOKING SOUTH. It lies above the Marble Hall and separates the State Apartments on the west front from those on the east front.

THE NORTH-EAST END OF THE PICTURE GALLERY. The paintings with which its walls are hung are mostly of the Dutch school and were collected by George IV.

34

THE THRONE DAIS IN THE BALL ROOM. This room was designed for Queen Victoria by Nash's pupil, James Pennethorne, but was redecorated for Edward VII.

THE BALL ROOM. Here are held the most important of State functions. Tiers of seats face one another across the parquetry floor, and at the opposite end to the Throne Dais is an organ.

THE BOW ROOM. It lies beneath the Music Room on the opposite side of the Marble Hall to the Grand Hall.

THE 1855 ROOM. The paintings commemorate the visit of Napoleon III and the Empress Eugénie to England in that year and Queen Victoria's reciprocal visit to France.

THE HOUSEHOLD DINING ROOM. The decoration was designed by Nash and has never been altered.

THE SOUTH END OF THE PRINCIPAL CORRIDOR IN THE EAST FRONT. The portrait of Queen Victoria
above the looking-glass doors is by Sir George Hayter.

THE APPROACH TO THE ROYAL BALCONY. This is the view the Royal Family sees on stepping out on to the balcony on great State occasions. Beyond the Victoria Memorial is a vista down the Mall to the Admiralty Arch.

WINDSOR CASTLE

It is significant that the Royal Family should now be called the House of Windsor, for Windsor Castle is the Crown's most ancient and historic palace and has been a Royal possession since about 1070, when William the Conqueror established a fortress there as one of a ring of castles to protect London. Even before the Norman Conquest there had been a Saxon palace on the River Thames at Windsor, but William the Conqueror abandoned this low riverside residence and built his new citadel on the higher ground where it still stands. The site was easily defensible, being on a steep open hill, with the Thames providing a natural barrier to the north and east. Later monarchs gradually improved the fortifications of the old Norman castle, and their successors transformed it from a fortress into the palace that we see today straddled magnificently along its commanding ridge.

Windsor Castle is shaped like an hour-glass. At its narrow neck in the Middle Ward stands the Round Tower, surmounting the earthen mound which marks the position of William the Conqueror's shell keep and separates the Lower Ward on the west from the Upper Ward on the east. In the Lower Ward stand St George's Chapel and its appendages, and round the Upper Ward —known as the Quadrangle—are grouped the buildings that comprise the Sovereign's residence. The outline of the three wards is the same now as it was in Norman times, except that then the defences were constructed of wood and earth. Henry II replaced the wooden palisades with walls of stone, and his grandson, Henry III, completed the circuit and punctuated it with numerous towers in the thirteenth century. Henry III also built a chapel in the Lower Ward, which in 1348 became the focus of the Order of the Garter, recently founded by Edward III. This monarch was born in the Castle—he was known as Edward of Windsor—and he made many additions to it, notably the Royal quarters in the Upper Ward.

St George's Chapel was begun by Edward IV, superseding Henry III's old chapel. It is one of the most beautiful ecclesiastical buildings in England and a masterpiece of Perpendicular architecture. The chancel is primarily the Chapel of the Order of the Garter, but many English sovereigns since Henry VI have been buried there. St George's Chapel took fifty years to build: it was unfinished when Edward IV died and was completed by Henry VII, who further extended the Royal quarters in the Upper Ward.

On the whole the Tudor and early Stuart monarchs did little to Windsor, and it was not until the reign of Charles II that the Castle received further Royal attention. In 1670, according to the diarist John Evelyn, it was 'exceedingly ragged and ruinous', and Charles II, inspired perhaps by the palaces he had seen abroad during his exile, resolved to rebuild the Royal apartments while—a sign of the times—the defences were also put in order. Many of the buildings in the Upper Ward were demolished, and in their place arose the resplendent State Apartments designed by Hugh May. Resplendent within, but not without: for from the outside they had originally a somewhat monotonous and far from castle-like—not to say dull—appearance. But that was rectified later. Their present romantic character dates from the 1820s, when the Castle underwent its next great reconstruction at the instigation of George IV. In the intervening period the buildings had deteriorated and the accommodation left much to be desired, although George III had made his home there at intervals after 1778 and had begun—with James Wyatt as his architect—to put the domestic quarters in order. George III's tentative work was engulfed by that of his son, who between 1824 and 1828 completely transformed the Upper Ward. His architect was Jeffry Wyatt, nephew of James Wyatt, who on the day that the foundation-stone of the new work was laid was authorized to change his name to Sir Jeffry Wyatville. A contemporary wit pleaded:

Let George, whose restlessness leaves nothing quiet,
Change if He must the good old name of Wyatt;
But let us hope that their united skill
Will not make Windsor Castle Wyatt Ville.

The plea was unfulfilled. Windsor Castle—or at least the Upper Ward—is largely Wyatville. Architecturally the exterior is hard to admire, and its texture and detail are at once coarse and affected; but there can be no doubt that this great stone pile, with its crenellated skyline and numerous towers, satisfies the romantic notion of a castle to a much greater extent than the homely boxes of the Caroline building that it swallowed up. Moreover, the interior is magnificently decorated, as we shall see, and the construction of the Castle has remained sound and firm to this day.

Entry to the Castle is by King Henry VIII's Gateway, into the south-west corner of the Lower Ward. Facing the visitor is St George's Chapel, behind which, strung along the west and north walls of the Ward, are the picturesque series of buildings associated with the Chapel: the Horse-Shoe Cloisters, the Chapter Library, the Canons' Cloisters and the Dean's Cloisters. To reach the Sovereign's residence in the Quadrangle one turns to the right inside the Gateway, and walks uphill past the mediæval and Tudor Lodgings of the Military Knights—retired officers of distinction—which are built along the south wall of the Lower Ward. On one's left, prolonging eastwards the line of St George's Chapel, is the Albert Memorial Chapel, which was rebuilt by Queen Victoria incorporating part of Henry III's old chapel. Ahead looms the Round Tower—which is not a true circle—and here the hand of Wyatville is plainly discernible, for he doubled the height of the original structure by raising the walls another thirty feet and surmounting them with machicolation. The Round Tower is thus largely a piece of scenery on a grand scale, but the added height makes it the hub and centre of the Castle, and it provides a dominating landmark for miles around.

The roadway skirts the north periphery of the ditch and mound of the Round Tower—now an unusual and cleverly planted garden—passes beneath the so-called Norman Tower—actually built by Edward III—and enters the Quadrangle, the outward appearance of which is due almost entirely to Wyatville. On the open side, backed by the grassy mound of the Round Tower, is Stada's equestrian statue of Charles II. On the east and south sides lie the Private Apartments, and on the north are the State Apartments, which are linked to the Norman Tower at their western end by Henry VII's building and Queen Elizabeth's Gallery. In the former's oriel window, looking northwards over the Thames, Queen Anne first heard the news of the Battle of Blenheim in 1704. Queen Elizabeth's Gallery now contains part of the Royal Library.

The State Entrance to Charles II's State Apartments is in the middle of the north façade of the Quadrangle, and is reached through the *porte cochère* under the clock tower erected by Wyatville. It opens into the State Entrance Hall, a vaulted chamber which survives from the domestic range built by Edward III. This gives on to the Grand Staircase, which was originally formed by Wyatville in an internal courtyard called Brick Court and received its present Gothic form in the 1860s when rearranged by Anthony Salvin. It contains a notable collection of armour and weapons, and on the half-landing stands Sir Francis Chantrey's marble statue of George IV. At the head of the Staircase one enters the State Apartments, which are regularly open to the public when the Court is not in residence. They are shown to visitors in the following order.

First, King Charles II's Dining Room, which remains much as Hugh May designed it in 1675, except that the filling in of Brick Court has deprived it of direct light. This, unfortunately, makes it difficult to see the superb decoration: the festoons carved by Grinling Gibbons to represent the fruits of earth, sea and air, and the painted ceiling by Antonio Verrio, depicting a Banquet of the Gods. Over the chimney-piece hangs a portrait of Charles II's Queen, Catherine of Braganza, by Huysmans, and there are also portraits by Mytens.

Beyond extend a series of intercommunicating State Apartments that face northwards and command a sweeping view across the valley of the River Thames. At one time all these rooms were decorated like the Dining Room, but the Verrio ceilings were all in bad condition—at least that was the excuse—when Wyatville restored the State Apartments in 1828, and he replaced them with the existing gilded ceilings. Gibbons's woodwork has also largely disappeared, although some of the rooms retain their original cornices. First in the series is the Rubens Room, in which hang a number of impressive paintings by or after Rubens. The only exception is Van Dyck's fine *St Martin dividing his Cloak with the Beggar*, hanging between the chimney-piece and the door into the adjoining State Bedroom. The latter is notable for the splendid Louis XVI bed, by Jacob, and for the assembly of paintings by or after Van Dyck. There follow the King's Closet, containing a number of seventeenth-century portraits, and the Queen's Closet, with its remarkable array of paintings by Canaletto, from which one reaches the Picture Gallery—the last Apartment on this front. In it hang paintings of distinction by a number of outstanding artists, including Clouet, Dürer, Memling, Andrea del Sarto, Holbein, Rubens, Rembrandt, Van Dyck and Claude. From the Picture Gallery one reaches the State Apartments overlooking the Quadrangle by way of the Van Dyck Room, which faces west towards the Norman Tower. Here are to be seen a number of portraits by or after Van Dyck, mostly depicting members of the family or Court of Charles I. Notable among them are the triple portrait of Charles I and the portrait-groups of his children. Also in this room is some of the famous silver furniture presented to Charles II and William III by the City of London, and examples of French eighteenth-century furniture.

The first Apartments in the range on the south, or Quadrangle, side are the Queen's Audience Chamber and the Queen's Presence Chamber, both of which retain their superb Caroline decoration and are among the most beautiful rooms at Windsor. Verrio painted the ceilings, in each of which Catherine of Braganza is the central figure, and Gibbons carved the surrounds to the pictures, which include works by Honthorst and Kneller. The late-eighteenth-century Gobelins tapestries in these Apartments depict incidents from the story of Ahasuerus

AERIAL VIEW OF WINDSOR CASTLE FROM THE WEST. In the foreground is the Lower Ward, containing St George's Chapel, one of the most beautiful ecclesiastical buildings in England. The Round Tower separates the Lower Ward from the Upper Ward, known as the Quadrangle, round which are grouped the State Apartments and the Private Apartments.

AERIAL VIEW FROM THE EAST, SHOWING THE QUADRANGLE AND ROUND TOWER. In the foreground is the East Terrace Garden, formed by George IV. The south and east sides of the Quadrangle contain the Private Apartments. The north side, facing across the River Thames towards Eton College Chapel, contains the State Apartments.

and Esther. Noticeable among the furniture is a set of late-seventeenth-century Venetian armchairs in the Presence Chamber.

It is a far cry from the restrained Caroline splendour of the Presence Chamber to the Gothic ebullience of the adjoining Guard Chamber—redecorated by Wyatville—which lies above the Grand Entrance with a projecting bay over the *porte cochère*. Here are displayed a number of interesting relics: they include the Elizabethan armour worn and used at a number of Coronations by the Champions of England; the bullet that killed Lord Nelson; and the banners submitted to the Sovereign each year by the Dukes of Marlborough and Wellington on the anniversaries of the Battles of Blenheim and Waterloo, by which service they hold their seats of Blenheim Palace and Stratfield Saye. Among the pictures that line the walls are works by Van Somer, Mytens and Lely.

On the opposite side of the Guard Chamber to the Queen's Presence Chamber is St George's Hall, which was formed by Wyatville from Charles II's Chapel and the original Hall built by Edward III in the fourteenth century. It is decorated in the Gothic taste with a row of tall arched windows overlooking the Quadrangle and a coffered wooden roof on which are painted the coats-of-arms of Knights of the Garter. Along the walls are ranged marble busts on pedestals—they include one of George II by Roubiliac—and above them portraits of Stuart and Hanoverian Sovereigns of the Order of the Garter alternate with trophies of arms and armour.

From St George's Hall the visitor turns northwards into the Grand Reception Room, which was fashioned by Wyatville out of Charles II's Guard Room and lavishly decorated in Rococo style, foreshadowing the State Apartments at Buckingham Palace. The gilded walls and ceiling provide a handsome background to the fine Regency furniture and the rich Gobelins tapestries depicting the story of Jason. In the bay window, which faces north, stands a malachite vase given to Queen Victoria by Nicholas I of Russia. The Grand Reception Room gives access to the Garter Room—which in turn communicates with the Rubens Room—and the Waterloo Chamber. The Garter Room is associated with the Order of the Garter: its carpet and upholstery are in the Garter blue and on its walls hang portraits of Sovereigns in their Garter robes. The room owes its decoration to Wyatville, but he incorporated panels and festoons carved by Gibbons which had formerly been in Charles II's Chapel.

The Waterloo Chamber is the largest of the State Apartments and is more impressive for its size and contents than for its architectural qualities. It was formed by Wyatville by roofing over an interior courtyard called Horn Court—just as he formed the Staircase in Brick Court—and is likewise lit from above. This great hall was designed to display George IV's magnificent collection of portraits—mostly by Lawrence—of the monarchs, prelates, statesmen, generals and admirals who collaborated to bring about the downfall of Napoleon. Here each year on June 18 is held the Waterloo Banquet. The decoration is mainly Victorian—it was designed by Edward Blore—and so is the immense seamless carpet, which was made for Queen Victoria by prisoners in India, but panels of carving by Gibbons were rescued from the Chapel by Wyatville and introduced into his original scheme.

From the Waterloo Chamber the visitor passes through the Grand Vestibule, which was formed by Wyatville in the place of the staircase built by his uncle James Wyatt for George III. It is lit from above by Wyatt's original lantern, which illuminates a display of military trophies, including relics of Napoleon, and George IV's Coronation robes. From the Grand Vestibule the visitor re-enters the Grand Staircase, and the tour of the State Apartments is at an end.

In 1778, when George III decided to use Windsor Castle as a residence, he chose for himself a suite of rooms facing north situated beneath the State Apartments, while Queen Caroline and their daughters were given rooms in the domestic quarters built by Edward III along the curtain wall of the south and east walls of the Upper Ward. When George IV began his renovation he chose that part previously occupied by his mother and sisters, and it was there that Wyatville rebuilt for him the existing Private Apartments.

The first problem was to ensure privacy. George III had allowed his subjects to wander at will into his garden, but George IV was more retiring and so Wyatville contrived the East Terrace Garden, which gives the appearance of being sunk, although in fact it is at the same level as the surrounding ground and the effect is obtained by the raising of the encircling terrace walk. The second problem was to provide a convenient entry to the Apartments, and this was overcome by building a three-sided *porte cochère* in the south-east corner of the Quadrangle. The third and most pressing problem was communication—George III had been forced to walk across the Quadrangle to visit his daughters. This Wyatville met by building a two-storeyed structure round the south and east sides: the ground floor provides offices and the first floor is taken up by the spacious Grand Corridor, over 500 feet in length, which serves as a magnificent picture gallery and gives access to the principal rooms of the Private Apartments.

The most notable of these are the three sumptuous drawing-rooms on the east front, facing across the Terrace Garden with a panoramic view towards London.

They are in Wyatville's most exuberant manner and provide a rich setting for their remarkable contents. In the White Drawing Room may be noted some superb examples of Louis XVI furniture and also the black doors, which came from Carlton House. From the same source came the chimney-piece in the Green Drawing Room, where may be seen portraits by Lawrence, Regency furniture, a pair of Chippendale mirrors and the famous blue Sèvres dinner service bought for George IV by his French pastrycook. The third Apartment in the series is the Crimson Drawing Room, in which hang portraits of King George VI and Queen Elizabeth the Queen Mother by Sir Gerald Kelly. Notable also are the portraits of George III's daughters by Beechey, the examples of Regency furniture, and the numerous magnificent doors, carved with symbols of the arts, agriculture and navigation, which came from Carlton House.

The junction of the south and east fronts of the building is marked by the Victoria Tower, which was rebuilt by Hugh May to provide accommodation for Charles II's brother, the Duke of York, and was later occupied by George III's consort, Queen Charlotte. Wyatville gave the tower its present castellated exterior and Queen Victoria gave it her name, for she chose it for her own apartments. These delightful rooms have been occupied by every subsequent Queen of England, and still serve the same function.

Along the south front Wyatville provided further apartments, notably that now called the Wedgwood Room and Queen Victoria's Audience Room, which received its present form during her reign and contains a series of portraits of her children by Winterhalter. Near the western end of this front Wyatville raised the twin York and Lancaster Towers, which were designed to provide a dramatic entrance to the Quadrangle from the Long Walk. This three-mile avenue of elms had been planted by Charles II and had reached maturity by the time that George IV began his transformation of the Castle. He found that the vista down the avenue was obscured by intervening buildings, but Wyatville demolished them and brought the Long Walk up to the walls of the Castle. In 1945 the trees had to be felled and replanted, owing to elm disease, but the Long Walk still provides a triumphal approach from the south, and as one gazes along its lines of growing trees towards the great Castle on its hill beyond, one can readily appreciate how Windsor has come to be regarded not only as the Sovereign's residence but also as a symbol of monarchy.

No description of Windsor Castle would be complete without a mention of Royal Lodge, the Sovereign's country house in Windsor Great Park. It was originally little more than a cottage, which was considerably enlarged for the Prince Regent by John Nash about 1812 and later extended by Wyatville. William IV pulled it down except for the Wyatville addition, the Georgian Gothic style of which inspired the existing building, designed by Mr Geoffrey Jellicoe for the Duke and Duchess of York in 1931. Even after the Duke's accession to the Throne as King George VI in 1936, Royal Lodge continued to be used for informal visits to Windsor, and it remains a favourite retreat of the Royal Family.

PANORAMIC VIEW OF THE CASTLE FROM THE SOUTH, SEEN OVER THE TOPS OF THE VENERABLE OAKS IN WINDSOR GREAT PARK

HENRY VIII's GATEWAY. This is the entrance to the Lower Ward. It was built in 1511 and provides the principal entrance to the Castle.

LOOKING ACROSS THE LOWER WARD TO THE ROUND TOWER. On the left is St George's Chapel; on the right, the lodgings of the Military Knights.

THE APPROACH TO THE TWIN YORK AND LANCASTER TOWERS FROM THE FOOT OF THE LONG WALK. This three-mile-long avenue was planted by Charles II in 1685, but had to be replanted in 1945.

47

THE NORMAN GATEWAY ON THE NORTH SIDE OF THE ROUND TOWER. It guards the approach from the Lower Ward to the Quadrangle.

EQUESTRIAN STATUE OF CHARLES II IN THE QUADRANGLE. It lies at the foot of the mound on which stands the Round Tower.

THE WEST END OF ST GEORGE'S CHAPEL. This masterpiece of the style of late Gothic architecture known as Perpendicular was begun by Edward IV and completed by Henry VIII.

THE ENTRANCE TO THE STATE APARTMENTS ON THE NORTH SIDE OF THE QUADRANGLE. The tall windows on the right light St George's Hall. On the left is the Round Tower, with Charles II's statue at its base.

THE SOUTH AND EAST FRONTS OF THE UPPER WARD, FROM THE HOME PARK. At the junction of the two fronts is the Victoria Tower, which was rebuilt for Charles II by Hugh May and altered by Sir Jeffry Wyatville for George IV. For more than a century it has provided apartments for the Queens of England.

THE EAST FRONT, FROM THE EAST TERRACE GARDEN. This front was originally a curtain wall, punctuated by watch-towers, but Edward IV lined it with living accommodation, and it was given its present battlemented appearance by Wyatville.

THE SOUTH FRONT. On the left are the York and Lancaster Towers, and on the right the Victoria Tower. Between the York and Lancaster Towers is King George IV's Gateway, from which a vista is obtained down the Long Walk.

THE CASTLE SEEN FROM ACROSS THE RIVER THAMES.   In front of the Round Tower is the Winchester Tower, where George IV's architect, Sir Jeffry Wyatville, lived while he was rebuilding the Castle.

THE STATE ENTRANCE HALL.   From this Hall the State Apartments are reached. The vaulting and columns date from the reign of Edward III, who rebuilt this part of the Castle.

THE HEAD OF THE GRAND STAIRCASE. It was designed by Anthony Salvin and completed in 1866. Below the marble statue of George IV, by Sir Francis Chantrey, stands a suit of armour made for Henry VIII.

KING CHARLES II's DINING ROOM. This is one of the few State Apartments that survive much as Hugh May designed them for Charles II. The ceiling, painted by Antonio Verrio, depicts a Banquet of the Gods; and wood carvings by Grinling Gibbons represent the fruits of earth, air and water.

KING CHARLES II's DINING ROOM. Over the marble chimney-piece, in a surround carved by Grinling Gibbons, is a portrait by Jacob Huysmans of Charles II's Consort, Catherine of Braganza.

THE EAST AND SOUTH WALLS OF THE RUBENS ROOM. It is so called because all the paintings in it except one are by Rubens. The principal furniture is of French origin, and the decoration, like that of most of the succeeding apartments, is due to Wyatville.

THE SOUTH AND WEST WALLS OF THE RUBENS ROOM. The painting to the right of the marble chimney-piece is the only one in the room not by Rubens: it is Van Dyck's *St Martin dividing his Cloak with the Beggar*.

THE KING'S CLOSET. The paintings that line the walls are mostly portraits of the seventeenth century. Through the open door there is a glimpse of the Picture Gallery beyond the Queen's Closet,

THE QUEEN'S CLOSET.   It contains a famous assembly of paintings by Canaletto, no fewer than fifteen in number.

THE VAN DYCK ROOM. It is hung with portraits of Charles I and members of his family and court. Over the chimney-piece is the famous triple portrait of Charles I, and on either side are portraits of Queen Henrietta Maria.

THE WEST WALL OF THE VAN DYCK ROOM. Between the middle windows are the pieces of silver furniture presented to Charles II and William III by the City of London. The door in the corner leads to the Queen's Audience Chamber.

THE STATE BEDROOM.   It lies between the Rubens Room and the King's Closet and is dominated by the superb canopied bed, which was made by the French cabinet-maker G. Jacob.

66

THE QUEEN'S AUDIENCE CHAMBER. Designed by Hugh May for the use of Catherine of Braganza, who is depicted being drawn in a chariot in Verrio's painted ceiling. The surrounds to the paintings over the doors were carved by Grinling Gibbons.

THE QUEEN'S PRESENCE CHAMBER. Like the adjoining Audience Chamber, this room retains its original Caroline decoration, with ceilings by Verrio and carving by Gibbons. The late-eighteenth-century Gobelins tapestries in both rooms represent the Bible story of King Ahasuerus and Queen Esther.

ARMOUR OF THE KING'S CHAMPION IN THE GUARD CHAMBER. This splendid suit of armour, made at Greenwich in Queen Elizabeth I's reign, was worn by the King's Champions at Coronations.

ST GEORGE'S HALL. The existing chamber was formed by Wyatville from Edward III's original hall and Charles II's chapel, which were thrown into one. On the ceiling are painted the coats-of-arms of Knights of the Garter, and on the walls hang portraits of Stuart and Georgian sovereigns of the Order of the Garter.

THE GRAND RECEPTION ROOM. This is one of the most sumptuous of the State Apartments redecorated by Wyatville for George IV, and links St George's Hall with the Waterloo Chamber. The malachite vase in the window was presented to Queen Victoria by Nicholas I of Russia.

THE WATERLOO CHAMBER. Formed out of an open courtyard by Wyatville to house George IV's collection of portraits of the principal monarchs, statesmen and soldiers who combined against Napoleon.

THE EAST AND SOUTH WALLS OF THE WATERLOO CHAMBER. Here each year on June 18, the anniversary of Napoleon's defeat by the Duke of Wellington at Waterloo in 1815, is held the famous Waterloo Banquet.

THE CORRIDOR, LOOKING EAST. The Corridor runs along the Quadrangle sides of the south and east fronts and serves the Private Apartments. The portrait on the right is of Sir Jeffry Wyatville.

THE GREEN DRAWING ROOM. One of the suite of three resplendent reception rooms on the east front, overlooking the East Terrace Garden.

77

THE CRIMSON DRAWING ROOM. State Portraits of Queen Elizabeth the Queen Mother and King George VI by Sir Gerald Kelly flank the chimney-piece embrasure.

78

THE WHITE DRAWING ROOM. Between the black doors, which came from Carlton House, stands the cabinet of the Comte d'Artois, one of the finest pieces of furniture in the Royal collection.

KING GEORGE VI's SITTING ROOM

80

THE QUEEN'S SITTING ROOM

81

THE PALACE OF HOLYROODHOUSE

HOLYROODHOUSE, Edinburgh, is the ceremonial Royal residence in Scotland, though it has, of course, been used only at intervals since James VI of Scotland became James I of England.

The historic Palace of the Scottish Kings lies at the east end of Canongate, where Edinburgh ends and the open country that culminates in the towering Arthur's Seat begins. Legend has it that King David I was hunting near by in defiance of the fact that it was a holy day and narrowly escaped being impaled on the antlers of a stag at bay, which was startled into flight 'by the apparition of a luminous Cross in the sky'. In thanksgiving for his escape the King founded the Abbey at Holyroodhouse in 1128, and lavishly endowed it. Most of the original monastic buildings have disappeared, but the ruined Abbey church adjoins the Palace to the north-east.

The Palace was begun by James IV, who built the sturdy tower that faces the visitor at the end of Canongate. His successor, James V, enlarged the Palace, but a considerable part of it was destroyed by fire in 1544 during the expedition known as the Rough Wooing, when an English force commanded by the Earl of Hertford invaded Scotland in retaliation for the broken marriage treaty between Henry VIII's son, Edward, and the infant Mary Stuart. When the young Princess returned to Scotland from France as Queen of Scots the Palace had been rebuilt, partly with stone from the old Abbey buildings. Both James I and Charles I put the Palace in order, but during the Commonwealth it was used as a barracks and again badly damaged by fire.

As it stands today, Holyroodhouse is due largely to Charles II, his architect, Sir William Bruce of Balcaskie, and his master mason, Robert Milne. James IV's Tower

—in which Mary Queen of Scots saw her secretary David Rizzio dragged to his death—was almost all that survived of the original Palace; Sir William balanced it by a second tower and between the two he built a screen, through which one enters the Quadrangle. The buildings surrounding this are of three storeys, with a Doric arcaded ground floor, Ionic first floor and Corinthian second floor. The State Rooms in this part of the Palace are admirable examples of the Charles II period, notable for their panelled walls and plaster ceilings. They include the Picture Gallery, which is decorated with curious portraits of more than a hundred Scottish Kings.

Charles II was never able to visit the Palace himself, but he took a personal interest in its reconstruction and among other things insisted that such rebuilding as had been done during the Commonwealth should be demolished. During his reign it was occupied by his brother, the Duke of York, who was the last member of the Royal Family to reside there for any length of time. The Palace had other Royal occupants at intervals, however. In 1745 Bonnie Prince Charlie paid it a brief though festive visit, but the next year it was to receive his conqueror, the Duke of Cumberland. After the French Revolution, Louis XVIII was given hospitality there, and it was also the home in exile of another French monarch, Charles X, who found refuge there not only from his subjects but also from his creditors.

George IV visited Holyroodhouse in 1822 and Queen Victoria occasionally stayed there on her way to and from Balmoral. Latterly the Palace has been used as a residence when the Sovereign has paid an official visit to Scotland, and each year garden parties are held there by the Sovereign's Representative in Scotland.

THE SOUTH AND EAST FRONTS OF THE PALACE, WITH THE ABBEY ON THE RIGHT

THE PALACE FROM THE NORTH-WEST. Beyond, the towering landmark of Arthur's Seat.

THE ENTRANCE FRONT. The balustraded screen, through which is the entrance to the Quadrangle, was the latest of the building carried out for Charles II by his architect, Sir William Bruce.

83

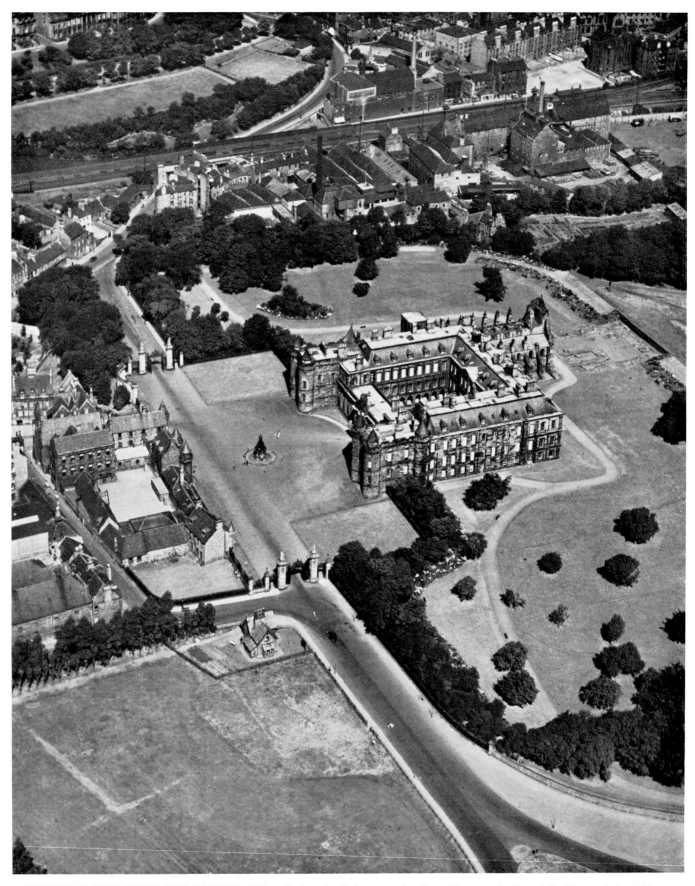

HOLYROODHOUSE FROM THE AIR. Facing the Palace are the Guard-house, the Royal Stables and the Abbey Court-house. The fountain in the forecourt is a Victorian copy of the fine fountain at the Palace of Linlithgow.

ENTRANCE TO THE FORECOURT. The forecourt was enclosed as part of the national memorial to King Edward VII, in whose memory the great wrought-iron gates were erected.

85

QUEEN MARY'S BEDROOM. It was from a small room next to this that David Rizzio was dragged from the Queen's presence and murdered in 1566.

QUEEN MARY'S AUDIENCE CHAMBER. The coffered ceiling displays the arms of the Queen and her first husband, the Dauphin of France, together with those of other members of the French and Scottish Royal Houses.

LORD DARNLEY'S AUDIENCE CHAMBER. One of the three rooms in the older part of the Palace that were used by Darnley during his marriage to Mary Queen of Scots.

THE PICTURE GALLERY. It contains the portraits of a hundred and eleven Scottish Kings painted for Charles II by the Dutch artist Jacob de Wet.

STATE ROOM, FORMERLY KNOWN AS QUEEN VICTORIA'S BEDROOM. The tapestries which adorn the State Apartments are of the late sixteenth and seventeenth centuries, and were woven in Paris and the Low Countries.

THE WEST DRAWING ROOM. The rich plasterwork of the ceilings in the State Rooms is by the two seventeenth-century English craftsmen George Dunserfield and John Houlbert.

THE GRAND STAIRCASE. It provides a ceremonial approach to the principal floor of the State Apartments.

89

ANOTHER VIEW OF 'QUEEN VICTORIA'S BEDROOM'

STATE ROOM, FORMERLY PRINCE ALBERT'S DRESSING ROOM. The enrichments of the overmantels, here as elsewhere, were the work of the Dutchman Jan Vansantvoort.

STATE ROOM, FORMERLY KNOWN AS QUEEN VICTORIA'S BREAKFAST ROOM

THE THRONE ROOM. The State Apartments are those used by the Sovereign when in residence at Holyroodhouse. They were redecorated and refurnished in the 1930s.

ST JAMES'S PALACE

IN 1698, the old Palace of Whitehall was burnt down, and the titular headquarters of the Sovereign's Court was transferred to St James's Palace, where it remains to this day. Foreign ambassadors are still accredited to, and Royal proclamations issued from, 'The Court of St James's'. Yet, considering the centuries of pomp and ritual implicit in this phrase, the origin of the Palace was incongruous enough. Early in the Middle Ages a pious Londoner founded a hospital for leprous women and dedicated it to St James the Less. As the disease had become almost extinct in the fifteenth century, Henry VI granted the buildings to his newly established College of Eton for the Provost to use as a London residence.

Henry VIII exchanged it with the College for other property in 1531 and, probably to please his second wife, Anne Boleyn, rebuilt it as a small palace, while at the same time he laid out the swampy ground to the south as a park. The two courts that form the core of the existing Palace are due to him. Among their features that still survive little altered are the Clock Tower, facing up St James's Street, and the Chapel Royal; in the chimney-piece to the Old Presence Chamber the initials of Henry VIII and Anne Boleyn, entwined in a true lovers' knot, can still be seen. No sooner was the building completed, however, than the unfortunate Queen was beheaded, after which the new Palace was rarely used. But St James's was the favourite residence of Queen Mary, and later James I appointed it to be the home of his eldest son, Prince Henry, for whom additions and alterations were made. Charles I redecorated certain rooms, and introduced the Mortlake tapestries that still hang in the Old Presence Chamber.

It is to Charles II that St James's Palace owes most, however, for during his reign Sir Christopher Wren added the beautiful Staircase and formed the long range of State Apartments overlooking the Park, in which Grinling Gibbons executed some of the carved decoration. Charles II's interest in the Palace and Park made the vicinity of St James's a fashionable residential neighbourhood, and though he did not occupy the Palace himself, his brother, the Duke of York, had his own Court there, and it continued to be his favourite residence after his accession to the Throne as James II. It was there that his son the Old Pretender was born—smuggled in by a warming-pan as the gossips said—and it was from there that he fled at the approach of William of Orange's Dutch Guards in 1688.

William III disliked St James's and he granted the Palace to his sister-in-law, afterwards Queen Anne, who had been born, baptized and married there. George I preferred Kensington Palace, but on George II's accession the Office of Works altered some of the State Apartments at St James's and enlarged the staircase. After 1763 George III lived principally at Buckingham House, but St James's continued to be used for all ceremonial occasions. The last important domestic event to take place there was the birth of George IV in 1762.

Much of St James's was burnt down in 1809, and after his accession George IV commissioned John Nash to restore the Palace and redecorate Wren's State Apartments. Their ceilings were heightened at the expense of the attic storeys above them, and much gilded decoration was introduced. The burning of the east range enabled the existing way through from the Park to Pall Mall to be formed, though it was not opened to the public until 1856.

No sooner had Nash finished his renovation of the Palace than George IV announced that he would transfer the Court functions to the new but still incomplete Buckingham Palace. St James's remains, however, the traditional Court of the Sovereign and the scene of many Court ceremonies.

AERIAL VIEW FROM THE SOUTH-EAST. St James's Palace is in the middle, with Clarence House abutting on to its western end. Marlborough House is in the lower right-hand corner. In the foreground is the Mall and in the background the Green Park, with St James's Street running northwards from the Clock Tower to Piccadilly.

THE STATE APARTMENTS ON THE SOUTH FRONT OF THE PALACE. They were added to Henry VIII's original building by Sir Christopher Wren in Charles II's reign, but were subsequently altered.

THE CLOCK TOWER AND GATEWAY. The view is from the bottom of St James's Street. This part of the Palace has been little altered since it was built by Henry VIII.

COLOUR COURT, LOOKING TOWARDS THE GATEWAY. On the left is the Chapel Royal, which was built about 1531. The colonnade was added by Sir Christopher Wren.

95

THE GRAND STAIRCASE.   The original Staircase was designed by Wren, but it was duplicated in George II's reign. At its head is a full-length portrait of Charles II by Peter Nason.

THE CHIMNEY-PIECE IN QUEEN ANNE'S DRAWING ROOM.   Above it hangs an equestrian portrait by David
Morier of George II, the last English monarch to appear in person at the head of his troops on the field of battle.

LOOKING FROM QUEEN ANNE'S DRAWING ROOM INTO THE DRAWING ROOM.
The handsome doors were designed by Wren, but their gilt decoration is of later date.

THE DRAWING ROOM. The portrait of William IV over the chimney-piece is flanked by four fine portraits of British Admirals by Reynolds and Hoppner.

THE THRONE ROOM, SHOWING THE THRONE BENEATH ITS CANOPY. Above the chimney-piece is a portrait of George IV, flanked by Grinling Gibbons carving.

THE OLD PRESENCE CHAMBER, OR TAPESTRY ROOM. In the chimney-piece are the initials of Henry VIII and Anne Boleyn, joined by a true lovers' knot.

CLARENCE HOUSE

At the western end of the range of State Apartments added by Wren to St James's Palace lies Clarence House. It was built originally in the seventeenth century and was one of the group of apartments, stables and offices that caused St James's to be described as 'like the Tower of London, a little town in itself'. Towards the end of the eighteenth century it was occupied by George III's third son, afterwards King William IV, who had been created Duke of Clarence in 1789.

These apartments were small and not in the least elaborate, though they were quite adequate for the simple tastes of the bachelor Duke. In 1824, however, six years after his marriage to Princess Adelaide of Saxe-Coburg-Meiningen, the Duke told George IV of the 'inconvenience and unfitness' and 'wretched state and dirt of our apartments'. It was a propitious moment to complain, as the Brighton Pavilion was almost finished and Buckingham Palace had not been begun, and the King authorized John Nash to rebuild the Duke of Clarence's Apartments. The work, begun in 1825 and finished two years later, was not accomplished without the financial troubles so often experienced by those who employed Nash. The building was subsequently altered both inside and out, but the part of Clarence House facing west towards Stafford House is due largely to Nash, and incorporates part of the original seventeenth-century apartments, which were not completely demolished.

The Duke of Clarence had been using his house for only three years when George IV died and the Duke became King. It was suggested that he should transfer his quarters to Marlborough House, which was then vacant, and for a short time he lived in St James's Palace, but eventually he returned to Clarence House and there he remained until the end of his reign. After his death in 1837 Clarence House had a number of occupants, including Queen Victoria's mother, the Duchess of Kent, but in 1866 it was granted to the Queen's second son, who had been created Duke of Edinburgh earlier in the same year. Clarence House then assumed more or less the appearance that it presents today. Although the Duke employed no architect—the alterations were designed by his builder, Mr Charles Waller—the late classical style of the additions harmonizes so well with Nash's original work that it is not easy to tell where one begins and the other ends. To Waller is due that part of Clarence House which links the original building to St James's Palace, and he was responsible for moving the entrance from the west front to its existing position on the south, where it is marked by an effective Tuscan portico.

The Duke of Edinburgh died in 1900, and until 1940 Clarence House was the London residence of Queen Victoria's youngest son, the Duke of Connaught. During the war it was the headquarters of the Red Cross and St John organization and so it remained until 1947, when it was announced from Buckingham Palace that 'Clarence House has been selected as the future official home of Her Royal Highness The Princess Elizabeth and Lieutenant Philip Mountbatten, R.N.'

The house was in a rather dilapidated state when it was taken over by Their Royal Highnesses. The bathrooms, electric-light system and service quarters were totally inadequate, and their provision accounted for much of the sum granted by the Government for the restoration of the house. When these necessary works had been carried out, little of the grant was left for the redecoration of the rooms. Successive alterations had largely obliterated their original late Georgian character, except for those rooms on the west front where Nash's ceilings and cornices survive, but a scheme of decoration has been devised that is both contemporary in feeling and simple in taste. As Mr Christopher Hussey wrote in the introduction to his *Clarence House* (1949): 'The foremost impression that a visitor now receives is of the charming, friendly, and quite informal home of a great lady'. This is borne out by the photographs accompanying these pages, which were taken before the death of King George VI. Clarence House is now the London residence of Queen Elizabeth the Queen Mother.

THE SOUTH FRONT, FROM THE GARDEN.   The left-hand portion of the building was built by John Nash for William IV when he was Duke of Clarence, but the portico and right-hand side are Victorian.

THE WEST FRONT IN PERSPECTIVE.   This façade is much as Nash designed it, except that the principal entrance has been removed to the south front.

THE ENTRANCE PORTICO. Beyond it are the State Apartments of St James's Palace.

THE WEST FRONT. The view from an archway of the colonnade in Stable Court.

103

THE DINING ROOM. It contains a series of portraits of members of the Royal Family at the time of George III, which appear to have hung there since Clarence House was occupied by the Duke of Clarence.

THE PRINCIPAL ENTRANCE

THE DRAWING ROOM ON THE FIRST FLOOR. This photograph was taken soon after the room had been redecorated and furnished for the Queen—or Princess Elizabeth as she then was—following her marriage to the Duke of Edinburgh.

DRAWING ROOM CHIMNEY-PIECE

BALMORAL CASTLE

In the autumn of 1847, Queen Victoria and the Prince Consort took a yachting holiday on the west coast of Scotland, and for five weeks it rained almost uninterruptedly. During the same period the son of their Physician-in-attendance, Sir James Clark, was staying at Balmoral, on Deeside; in his correspondence with his father he wrote continually of the fine weather that he was enjoying there, and Sir James reported this to the Queen. As a result she ordered an enquiry to be made into the climate and rainfall of Deeside, and it was found to be one of the driest areas in Scotland. In the following year, owing to the sudden death of Sir Robert Gordon, Balmoral Castle became available, and, apparently at Sir James Clark's suggestion, the Queen took over the lease of the house.

In 1852, when the lease acquired by Sir Robert Gordon expired, the Prince Consort bought the Balmoral estate for £31,500 from the trustees of the Earl of Fife, whose predecessors had bought the property in 1798 but had never lived there. Next year the Castle, which in 1834 had replaced an earlier structure, was pulled down, since it was too small to accommodate the Royal Family, and the existing Castle was erected on a neighbouring site.

Balmoral is built of granite in the style known as Scottish Baronial, with a picturesque roof-line dominated by a stout turreted tower. It was designed by the Prince Consort himself, with the professional assistance of Mr William Smith, city architect of Aberdeen. The interior was treated in extremely plain taste, in which a large part was played by sporting trophies and tartan curtains, carpets and upholstery: 'the fact was insisted on that this was no palace, but simply a royal shooting-box in the Highlands. There were to be no valuable oil-paintings and no lavish decoration; only comfort and economy were to be considered'. The Castle was completed and occupied in 1855, and in the following year the Queen wrote in her diary: 'Every year my heart becomes more fixed in this dear Paradise, and so much more so now, that *all* has become my dear Albert's *own* creation, own work, own building, own laying out, as at Osborne; and his great taste, and the impress of his dear hand, have been stamped everywhere'.

After the Prince Consort's death in 1861 Queen Victoria resided increasingly at Balmoral, and enlarged the estate by the acquisition of Ballochbuie Forest. Balmoral was so far from London that it was usual for a member of the Cabinet to be in attendance—'doing service' as Lord Palmerston called it—when the Queen was in residence there. This custom has for some time been suspended, and the Royal Family can now enjoy in comparative seclusion the recreations, air and views of what has come to be called Royal Deeside.

THE CASTLE IN ITS MAGNIFICENT SETTING, SEEN FROM THE NORTH

AERIAL VIEW FROM THE WEST, SHOWING THE CASTLE IN RELATION TO THE RIVER DEE. Balmoral was built in the style of architecture known as Scottish Baronial in 1853, and was designed by the Prince Consort himself.

THE SOUTH FRONT, WITH THE MAIN ENTRANCE ON THE LEFT AND THE TOWER ON THE RIGHT

THE NORTH AND WEST FRONTS

THE APPROACH TO THE CASTLE FROM THE SOUTH-EAST

CRATHIE CHURCH, WHERE THE ROYAL FAMILY WORSHIP WHEN THEY ARE AT BALMORAL

BALMORAL CASTLE: THE APPROACH TO THE MAIN ENTRANCE, FROM THE WEST

SANDRINGHAM HOUSE

SANDRINGHAM, in Norfolk, is the personal property of the Sovereign. In the middle of the nineteenth century it belonged to the gifted but unfortunate Countess D'Orsay. Shortly before his death in 1861 the Prince Consort bought the estate for his eldest son, the Prince of Wales, afterwards Edward VII, the purchase money of £220,000 being provided by the savings accumulated during the Prince's minority.

The estate of about 7,000 acres consisted largely of sandy, pine-studded heath, which has since been converted into well-timbered agricultural land, traversed by the breezes of the not-far-distant sea. The original early-nineteenth-century house was pulled down after its acquisition by the Prince of Wales and rebuilt in its existing form to the designs of Albert Jenkins Humbert, an architect who had first attracted the attention of the Prince Consort by his work on Whippingham Church, Isle of Wight.

Sandringham was built during an unfortunate period of English architecture, and the many-gabled brick-and-stone house does not appeal to the taste of the present day, but it has been truly said that it 'possesses one supreme virtue: it abounds in large windows which can be thrown wide open to fill the rooms with air and sun—the fresh, bracing air of north-west Norfolk, perfumed in summer with the scent of lawns and roses and pines'. The rooms are unassuming and comfortable, and appropriate to a country house of which the purpose is that it should be a contrast to the historic magnificence of Buckingham Palace and Windsor.

The charm of Sandringham lies in the gardens and surroundings—the farms, the stud, the village with its pretty collegiate buildings erected by successive 'Squires of Sandringham'. King Edward VII devoted the large winnings of his famous Derby winner Persimmon—whose statue stands in the stud farm—to this transformation of Sandringham. His successors have carried on the work, so that the splendidly managed estate is one of the most beautiful in England, besides being famous for the excellent shooting it affords.

THE GARDEN FRONT. Sandringham was built in the 1860s for Edward VII when Prince of Wales.

AERIAL VIEW SHOWING THE ENTRANCE FRONT, WITH THE GARDEN AND HOME PARK BEYOND

112